LEXICON

OF LIFE

IOANNIS TZIVANAKIS

LEXICON

OF LIFE

ITV

Content

For My Parents

Introduction

What makes us content? And what is content-ment itself?

What are emotions? And what exactly is fulfill-ment?

What do we want in life? And what does life mastery consist of?

What do we need in life? And what are life skills?

How does reality tick? What is the contribution of science?

What is understanding itself? Why is it so valuable?

In over six hundred definitions in the second part of this book we find answers to all these questions and gain insights into the basic building blocks of reality, into the most important life skills, into essential human characteristics, into central aspects of human existence and into key elements of life, knowledge and action.

The important aspects and dimensions of our life as well as the paramount role of understanding everything that life itself communicates and could still communicate to us, the context in which all word entries are embedded, is the subject of the first part of the book.

PART I

The Meaning Of Life

1. The Unique Miracle Of Life

Life is a miracle. Isn't it?

Seeing life as a miracle does not have to mean that life is always a beautiful event or always an easy existence.

Likewise, it does not mean that life is always something difficult or sorrowful.

But a miracle it is in any case. Both in where it comes from, how it comes about or through what it arises, under which conditions it flourishes or withers, and in that it is there at all, that it exists at all.

In the same way, all this is also true for the whole world, for the whole manifestation, as Wittgenstein (next page) appropriately states.

And here we are. Along with all our fellow lifers. And participate in it. In life. We are participants in this happening, in this existence, in this stream of being and especially feeling.

Because, between us: without the ability to feel, without the ability to sense, we can't experience life, can we?

Is therefore this feeling, this sensing the true

"1.   The world is everything that is the case.

1.1   The world is the totality of facts, not things.

....

2.   What is the case, the fact, is the existence of states of affairs.

2.01   The state of affairs is a connection of objects (entities, things).

....

6.44   Not how the world is, is the mystical, but that it is."

Ludwig Wittgenstein

miracle? And of course over and over again the challenge?

Isn't the only possible answer to this a yes? Aren't these questions only to be answered in the affirmative? For how are they to be negated? And isn't this yes the easiest answer to them, since it is so self-evident?

Agreed. It does not need a great deal of thought, if we have lived for a while and have experienced this, in order to be certain that this yes is right.

Mentally and tested by the mind, such a yes is simple and easy.

But is saying yes to life as a whole just as simple and easy? Very probably or certainly not. Because life as a whole gives us not only good, beautiful or reasonably bearable moments and phases, but very often also very difficult or quite sorrowful ones.

To affirm life as a whole against such a background is perhaps or rather the easier or more possible, the more mature our life skills are and the deeper our life mastery is rooted in the laws of reality.

2. Life In An Encoded World

If we put the pieces of a puzzle, a picture puzzle for example, together correctly, they form a picture which then represents the solution of the puzzle. The content of this picture becomes instantly clear as soon as all or at least most of the pieces of the picture are put together correctly, i.e. are arranged with each other as they belong together. The purpose of such a picture puzzle is that its content is revealed by spatially correctly structuring and arranging the picture components of which this content consists. This purpose is fulfilled at the moment when the picture is represented and revealed in its entirety.

The idea of a whole and its parts, which is inherent in a picture puzzle, can be found just as well in many other examples and areas. The same logic applies, for example, to a dish we want to prepare in such a way that the quality and flavor of the prepared food are consistent with our sense of taste.

However, if in the picture puzzle a picture reveals itself in its entirety by arranging the parts of the picture correctly together, then if we want to prepare a dish, we must both obtain the different foods, which in turn must be in a correct state, and determine the correct quantity for each food, proportionately, that is, in the correct ratio to the other ingredients. And then it may also need the right mixing or combining as well as the degree of cooking.

The activity of preparing a dish again contains the idea of a whole and its parts, but here the nature of the parts as well as the way the parts are put together to form a whole is quite different than in a picture puzzle.

Depending on the example or field, a whole is always that which determines both the nature of the necessary parts and the way in which these parts are brought together to form this whole. When we know what we want to achieve, when we know what whole must result, only then can we decide the right parts and the appropriate combination of these.

Because the whole can be something completely different in each case. It can be a garden. It can be a book. It can be an activity. It can be a group of people or other entities. It can be an organization. It can be a school. A business. A family. A village, a city, a country. But it can also be an argument. A condition, too. Or a schedule. A strategy. Or a relationship. It can be anything.

So that a whole, whatever the whole is, can result, a corresponding arrangement is always necessary. And an arrangement is <u>the certain way of the composition of all elements in a system, i.e. in a whole, and their relations to each other</u>.

Now, if life as a whole is what we are concerned with, then it is inevitably important to know and understand most, or preferably all, of the elements or parts that are necessary for a more or less mastered and fulfilled life.

When the state of these elements is in the proper condition and these elements are put together in the proper relationship, the result is a fulfilled life.

A fulfilled life occurs when all that takes place for which this life is intended by its self-fulfilling nature. As long as this life does not become what it is meant to be by its self-fulfilling nature and by its self-actualizing tendency, it is not yet fully "real" but partially realized and otherwise continues to be (only) a potential or possibility.

Once the coherent possibilities of a life have been unfolded and realized and have become what they were meant to be, such a life is a fulfilled reality. It is a fulfillingly realized life.

So what are the parts of this whole, this fulfilling and realized life?

And in what condition should they exist?

How must they be arranged and related to each other?

And what knowledge of the big and wide world and what skills in it are necessary for this?

3. Understanding As Decoding Ability

Every ordinary or normal moment contains all knowledge and can - under certain circumstances and if this knowledge is used - also fulfill every necessary condition for a life or existence that is self-nourishing and satisfying. With everything it needs in every moment.

However, all knowledge is of no use if we cannot tap into it or access it to nourish ourselves with it. Therefore, for a full or fulfilled life, we need, first, the necessary knowledge to do so and, second, the right circumstances.

According to Leibniz, we live in the best of all possible worlds because God is benevolent and he created the world.

According to Spinoza, it is possible to participate more and more in nature as a whole or in the divine - which for Spinoza is the same thing - or to become one with it, which is the highest or truest form of existence and means true peace.

In the case of Buddha or Schopenhauer, where even suffering is recognized as a basic feature of human existence, there is the way out of it, as soon

"Thus, I have a completely different opinion about God and Nature than that which ... is usually advocated. Namely, I conceive God as the inherent and not the external cause of all things. I plainly state that everything lives and weaves in God."

Benedictus de Spinoza

as we understand what is the matter and no longer chase the impossible, but let go of it or similar. But how does that work?

Regardless of the fact that my experience makes me feel closest to Spinoza, and regardless of these names of philosophy and spirituality, even if they are only a few of many and only the ones that come to mind, I can confirm how liberating, action-empowering and altogether enlightening the understanding of reality can be.

"Though the Logos (Universal Law)
is common, the many live as if they
had a wisdom of their own."

Heraclitus

Understanding in itself, whenever it takes place, is a fulfilling event. And this is not particularly surprising, because we are symbolic beings.

Everything we encounter has a meaning or even significance for us. Knowing or recognizing this meaning and significance through understanding is a contribution to the coherence and truth of what we experience. It always contributes to the relaxation of our state of mind and soul. Especially when it comes to understanding reality. Then everything just relaxes and lightens up.

This is not to say that mere understanding settles everything, no. Action is not left out by it. But through understanding, action also becomes clear in its why and in its how.

Isn't it relaxing to understand why we do something? Or why we want to do something or why we have to do something? Doesn't it give us clarity and peace?

Admittedly, understanding is not always easy. For example, it is very easy to understand when we think of the quantity or number of two things, apples for example, when we encounter the numeral 2. The number of two things is the correct meaning of the numeral or symbol 2, which stands for this

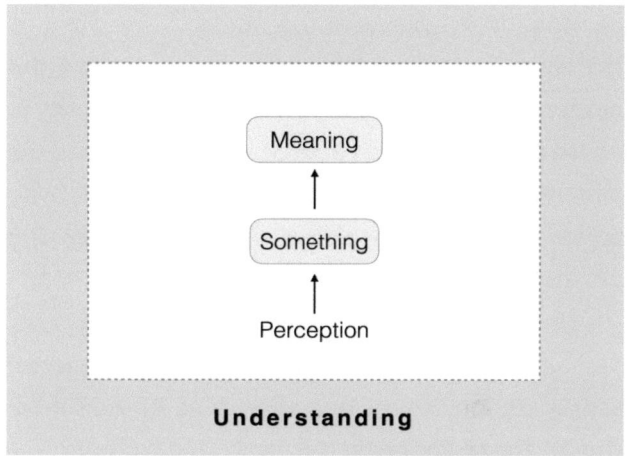

Understanding

very meaning.

More subtle, however, or at least more indirect and therefore more difficult, can be the understanding or, in this case, the interpretation, when we perceive and feel someone's unclear smile. Is friendliness meant? Or perhaps irony? Sometimes this is clear, sometimes not.

Often it is just as difficult to understand one's own emotions and what they mean, i.e. what causes them or what they are an expression of.

Even if understanding is not always easy or at least not immediately possible, always if we understand something, we carry out a double act of perception. So if I perceive the numeral 2 and immediately or instantaneously also the content of this numeral, thus the quantity two, then this quantity as content of the numeral is what I perceive behind the already perceived number. So I perceive something and at the same time I perceive what this something means.

When I perceive something and also perceive, feel or experience its content or meaning, its essence, its identity - very often also its reason or cause - then I understand it.

This applies to objects or things or also to relations between things. For example, one also understands a connection between a government policy and the satisfaction of the governed population. Or the connection of one person's actions and the effect of those actions on another person. Or the effect of food on how we feel. Or, or, or...

So, when we understand something, we are always dealing with the content, the real equivalent of one or more things, or the real equivalent of the relation or relationship between one or more things. The same is true of reality and us in it.

Moreover, it is important to distinguish both between objective and personal understanding and between further dimensions of understanding.

So, objectively, a tree can be a certain biologically constituted plant, but personally, it can mean oxygen or life to me, or rootedness in a figurative sense, or a symbol of the branching of a larger area into smaller ones, or even a certain emotion that arose in an intense experience associated with a tree. And so on.

Thus, what matters is not only what something is for itself or in itself or independently of everything else, but in the meaning it has for us; this meaning, in turn, depends on the perspective we take and from which we look at, perceive, sense, grasp and understand this very something.

Understanding is therefore multidimensional, multiperspectival and multilayered.

The ability of understanding is our main instrument for decoding life and reality. Everything we encounter, everything we experience feelingly or perceive at least to some degree, has a meaning or content only if we understand it.

Such understanding is indispensable mental, emotional and existential nourishment for a human organism. And such nourishment provides knowledge, enables growth and development, and gives inner satisfaction.

4. The Multiple Meaning Of The Fulfilled Life

All of reality, including our life, is a multidimensional totality or wholeness, a total fabric which consists of the interweaving of all its parts to each other and with each other.

The total fabric of reality and our life may be gigantic, inexhaustible in possible knowledge to be acquired and manifold in its different facets.

We must not lose ourselves in it, but by experiencing and understanding our life within the given reality, we must gain the clarity that comes from the realistic knowledge of the laws of reality and of being human.

The central or decisive ability to lead a more or less fulfilled life within these circumstances would be, to express it in a single word or rather expression, our life mastery, if by this is to be understood the sufficient, complete or very high ability to (a) to fulfill the necessities of life and (b) to realize as many valuable possibilities inherent in life as is feasible and appropriate.

It is no special realization or statement that there are necessities in life that have to be fulfilled, such as (a) a certain education and training, (b) the necessary social and emotional intelligence and (c) at least sufficient acquisition of everything that is purely materially necessary for life. We can also call all this basic life knowledge and skills.

If the basic life knowledge and skills are more or less assured, the pursuit of certain ideals or goals and the fulfillment of important needs, which in their totality contribute to a partial or more complete fulfillment of life, opens or activates. This in turn raises the following important question. How is life fulfillment defined, how does it open up to us? How do we notice it, or how do we measure it, that life is seen or rather experienced as being fulfilling? And what is the meaning of life? Or of our life? Or of my life?

This question can certainly be felt and asked consciously. But also unconsciously, at least most of the time, the actions, behavior and way of being of most is driven and moved by all that fulfills a smaller or larger meaning of life.

There may be disagreement among people as to what the meaning of life is.

For some, the meaning of life is to live according to a religious ideal.

For others, the meaning of life is to live on the basis of a philosophically or spiritually unlocked and revealed reality.

For others, the meaning of life is the meaning people give to themselves or find within themselves.

For others, the meaning of life is life itself, in our case human life itself in as many of its facets as possible to live, to be, to embody.

Let's leave it open, or let everything count, or a combination of everything or some. Only let us ask at least:

Does our consciously or unconsciously pursued purpose in life lead to a real sense and genuine experience of life fulfillment?

Does everything we do and how we are lead to contentment, freedom, wholeness and self-love or self-acceptance? To life fulfillment, in other words? Now? In the present?

5. The Essential Language Of Life

Reason, comprehension and general intelligence, and therefore knowledge, action and being, all this is not possible without a certain degree of language intelligence.

Language intelligence consists in mastering appropriate words and forms of expression to describe contents of thinking, feeling, experiencing, knowing and perceiving.

The more these contents relate to reality, to our lives and to the reality of our lives, the more relevant and therefore valuable is our language intelligence.

And language intelligence, when tested, confirmed and then embodied through experience, transforms into usable and exceedingly necessary life intelligence.

Such language intelligence is a treasure of knowledge and therefore also a treasure of life. It is the treasure of the words of life.

Such language intelligence contains knowledge about the basic building blocks of reality, about the most important life skills, about essential human characteristics, about central aspects of human existence and about key elements of life, knowledge and action.

Life is a miracle. And the whole of reality is just as much a miracle. Not only because it causes and triggers wonder in our feeling. It is a miracle because it is also a mystery.

Reality is a mystery in where it comes from or how it comes into being, and also in why it is the way it is.

With which language, i.e. with which language contents do reality and life speak to us? What do they tell us?

They tell us what we can perceive, experience, understand and live through with our entire human capacity.

And all this consists on the one hand of many millions of words.

On the other hand, however, there is a basic vocabulary. There is a basic and essential vocabulary of life.

This vocabulary of life contains the texture of reality. This vocabulary reflects life.

It contains the laws of the manifested existence as well as the spectrum of experience of the human being within its embeddedness in exactly this man-

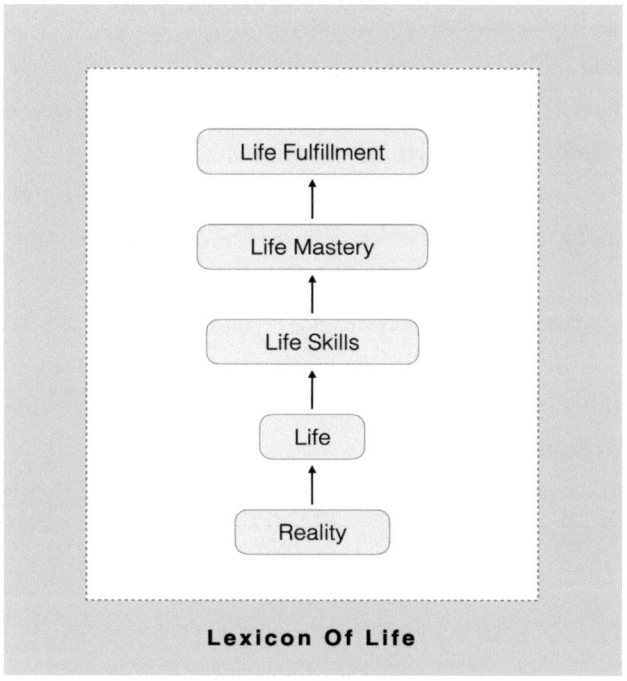

Lexicon Of Life

ifested existence.

It tells us quite clearly which life skills are central and decisive and in what life mastery consists and how it is achieved.

And it directly provides us with the knowledge of the prerequisites for life nourishment as well as the path to its fulfillment.

The essential vocabulary of life is there for us to use, so than we can become a complete and satisfied "part" of the wonder and mystery of life and reality and to exist in that state.

And since we are life itself, we are also automatically invited to honor and realize and embody this vocabulary of life. Not just to understand it.

Because understanding is beautiful. But to be something and to also understand it, and then to feelingly fully accept and embrace it, is the most beautiful of things.

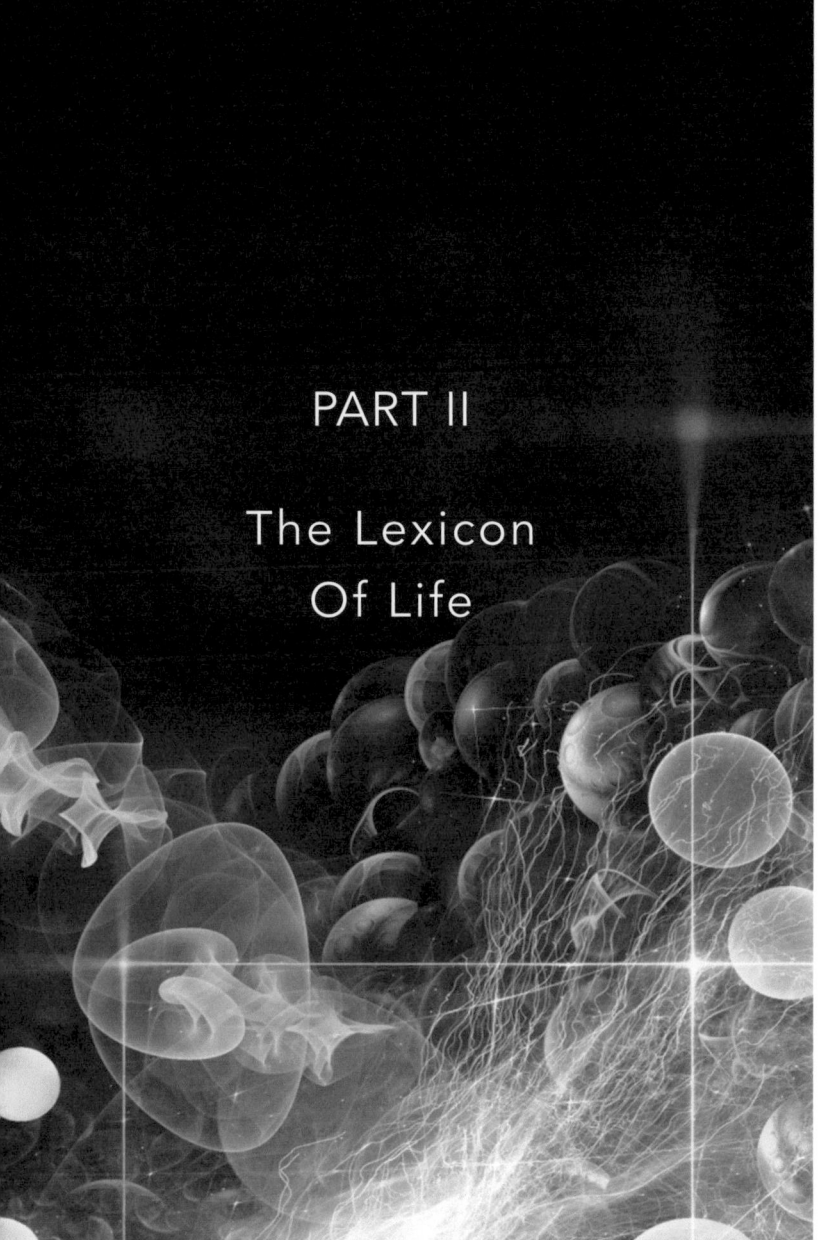

PART II

The Lexicon
Of Life

From **'ability'**

to **'culture'**

ability: possessing by nature or having internalized and embodying the physical or/and mental or/and emotional knowledge, and also having the power of doing or being something.

abstract: everything that cannot be perceived and experienced with the senses but with the mind.

achieve: to bring something to existence by being or doing.

act: to set and keep one's forces in purposeful motion.

action: psychophysical, usually purposeful application of organismic forces.

active: denotes the state of psychophysical and mostly purposeful application of organismic forces.

activity: psychophysical, mostly purposeful application of organismic forces.

actualize: to bring about, to bring into existence by certain application of certain forces.

actualizing tendency: the innate urge to unfold, re-alize and be what is inherently in us, as it is touched, nourished and dynamized by the natural laws of re-ality.

adult: a fully grown person, independent in life and responsible for his or her own actions.

affect: to cause a change in somebody or some-thing.

affection: the feeling state of wanting to come clos-er to something or wanting to be with something.

affirm: to feel or show affirmation for something.

affirmation: showing perception of something as correct or true.

after (1): shows something that follows something else in space.

after (2): shows something that is there or happens later than something else.

afterwards: shows something that follows some-thing else in time.

agitation: the feeling state of inner disturbance or/ and inner turmoil.

agreement: an interpersonal commitment to something that applies to and binds all involved parties.

alive: existing as a living being.

analysis: the activity or/and the process of perceiving, recognizing and understanding the content parts of something and their arrangement to each other.

analyze: to perceive, recognize and understand the content parts of something and their arrangement to each other.

application: the use of something to achieve something else or to make a process possible.

appropriate: the property of favoring and maintaining the essence or/and determination of the existence or and functioning of something.

arise: to come into existence.

arrange: to place, bring or put something in a location within a space or field or context according to its function.

arranged: the existing of something in a place or location according to its function within a space or field or context.

arrangement (1): the particular way of setting up all elements in a system and also their relations to each other.

arrangement (2): the way something is arranged or the way several or all parts of a whole are arranged.

art (1): activity to create anything that wants to or should cause reflection or the sensation of something beautiful.

art (2): the totality of all works for reflection or for the sensation of something beautiful.

artistic: belonging to art.

attention: directed consciousness.

attention intelligence: the experiential knowledge of the causes of movement and of the nourishing sources of one's attention.

authentic: belonging to the sensed real.

authenticity: the way of being that results from the respective sensed reality of all that expresses itself naturally and unhindered as our entire organismicity: as the "universe" of the energy flow of the perpetual cycle of being-sensing-needing-getting-becoming-being...

autonomous: free and independent to be, decide and act according to one's own principles and laws.

autonomy: the freedom and independence to be, decide and act according to one's own principles and laws.

autotelic: denotes a process or activity that is the goal of itself (auto = self, telos = goal).

aversion: the feeling of not wanting something to take place or of wanting to move away from something.

avoid: to not let something take place or to move away from something.

bad: something that interferes with or disturbs or is not at all appropriate for the fulfillment of a purpose.

be (1): to exist.

be (2): to indicate a quality or state.

be (3): to show the location of something or somebody.

beautiful: the quality of something perceived or experienced to cause in us satisfaction or/and euphoria or/and contentment.

beauty: the condition or composition of something, whose perception causes in us satisfaction or/and euphoria or/and contentment.

become: to come to a state or/and property by energy and force.

before (1): indicates something that comes or must come first in time or space in relation to something else.

before (2): shows that something is at the front of

something else.

begin: to come to the first moment of existence at a place or point in space or time.

beginning (1): the first of several parts of a process or entity.

beginning (2): the place, point in space or time before which something is not yet there.

behavior: the manner of acting (in the all-inclusive sense) and especially toward others.

behavioral intelligence: the knowledge and ability of appropriate being and acting in being with others.

being in the world: the existing and experiencing in the manifested total existence, which is the greatest in scope at any moment.

big: high degree of (usually) length.

biology: the investigation and study of true knowledge (a) of the composition of all living organisms and (b) of all laws and processes that regulate and govern living organisms.

bodily: of or pertaining to the body.

body: the connected totality of the form, structure and materiality of a living being.

boredom: the unpleasant deficient feeling state of lack of interest or/and excitement.

branch (1): the part of a tree that grows out of the main stem and on which twigs, leaves or needles and often flowers and fruits grow.

branch (2): one of several parts of an area or field or context.

breathe: to draw in and pour out the mixture of gases necessary for life.

bring: to move something to a place or to an area.

calculate: to find out how much something is when it is compared with something of its kind.

can: to have the ability.

capable: having the ability.

care: activity that has as its purpose the good or/ and pleasant happening or existence of a living being or of something else.

carry out: to (completely) cause a process from its beginning to its end.

category: group.

cause: a happening or an existing circumstance out of which something happens or comes to existence.

cause: to make something happen or come into existence by doing, behaving or being.

certain (1): something of which there is a strong feeling that it is as it is perceived or/and known to be.

certain (2): different in its properties from all other entities.

certainty: the strong feeling of the immutability of the knowledge about something.

chance: opportunity.

change (1): the process by which something becomes different.

change (2): the process by which something becomes different or new in time in its form or/and composition or/and quantity or/and arrangement.

change (3): quantitative or/and qualitative transformation or transformation of energetic arrangements or manifested configurations.

change: to cause the change of something.

character: the set of features and properties of something that distinguishes that something in its suchness from something similar.

characteristic: exhibiting the features and properties of something that distinguish that something in its suchness from something similar.

chemistry: investigation and study of true knowledge (a) of the nature of all elements and substances and (b) of all laws and processes that regulate and govern the behavior and transformation of elements and substances.

child (1): a person younger than an adult.

child (2): a person to whom other people fulfill the role of parents.

civilization (1): the totality of valuable accumulated knowledge with the purpose of good human coexistence.

civilization (2): through education emerged human way of being and living.

clarity: the state of perceiving or/and knowing or/and feeling in a fully obvious, undeniable and unclouded manner.

clear: directly and easily recognizable, perceptible, understandable and conceivable, precisely outlined, distinctive from something else.

closeness (1): at a small distance from something.

closeness (2): the feeling state of a more or less warm or/and intimate relationship with a living being.

cognize: to perceive something in its identity.

comfort: the feeling state of pleasant safety.

communicable: that which can be sent and/or received as information between sentient and cognitive beings.

communicate: to send or/and receive information.

communication: the happening in which information is sent and/or received between sentient and cognitive beings.

communicative intelligence: the experiential knowledge and the ability, based on it, to communicate appropriately and effectively and to deal with what is communicated.

communion: the experience of a feeling or state of oneness in being with one or more other living beings.

competence: the sufficient or high or very high degree of an ability to do something.

complete: whole.

complexity: the property of something to consist of some or more elements, which in turn are related or/and interact in one or more ways.

comprehensive: relating to a whole or to the whole of something.

compromise: the affirmation of the purposeful and reasonable restriction of one's own freedom or/and way of life and being.

compulsion: a force or condition that controls, influences or restricts us and does not arise from our freedom or our own free motivation.

conclude: to recognize something as a result of something else for specific reasons.

conclusion: recognizing something as a result of something else for specific reasons.

condition (1): that which is necessary for the happening or the existence of something else.

condition (2): state.

confusion: the feeling of disturbance of the mental

or/and emotional or/and overall energetic order.

connect: to bring two or more entities into a way of being together.

connected: to be in a connection or/and relationship with something else.

connection: a way of being together between two or more entities.

conscious: the mode of being that includes what is experienced in the knowledge of its facticity and is thus known by the experiencing I.

consciousness: the biological energy field that is the basis of all sensing or feeling for a living being.

consequence: that which is there or happens directly and exclusively as a natural or/and personally perceived result of something that is there or happens before.

consider: to think precisely in order to find out or/and understand something accurately.

construct: to create, to build up, to cause the coming into being of something.

contemplate (1): to think about something in inner collection and calmness.

contemplate (2): to meditate.

content (1): that which is contained in something else.

content (2): the meaning of something.

contentment: the state and feeling of nourishment, tranquility, wholeness and freedom.

control (1): the power over something.

control (2): the causing or/and directing of a way of being or happening of something.

control (3): overseeing the way something exists or happens.

control (1): to have power over something.

control (2): to cause or/and direct the way of being or happening of something.

control (3): to oversee how something exists or happens.

cosmos: the universe perceived as ordered.

courage: feeling the strength or/and ability to do something, which is perceived as difficult.

create (1): to bring something to material existence.

create (2): to bring something into existence by being or doing.

culture (1): the totality of all valuable human intellectual and artistic works.

culture (2): human way of being and living.

"The Present is always there, together with its Content: both stand firm without wavering; like the rainbow on the waterfall. For to the Will is Life, and to Life the Present, sure and certain."

Arthur Schopenhauer

From **'curiosity'**

to **'freedom'**

curiosity: the need to experience or/and know something.

cybernetics: the science of steering or directing (Greek: kyberno = to steer, navigate; Sanskrit: kubara = steering wheel of a means of motion).

danger: something possible or existent that can cause disturbance, pain or non-existence.

death: the irreversible event after which a living being no longer lives or/and exists.

decide (1): to commit to one of two or more possibilities of fulfillment of a need or necessity.

decide (2): to determine.

define: to identify or/and show the set of all characteristics that make something what it is.

definition: the set of all characteristics that make something what it is.

degree: the how much of the measure, strength or level of something on the scale of the corresponding field.

dependent: something that has no self-existence or needs something else as the cause of its existence.

determine: to cause the way of being or happening of something.

determined: caused to be or happen in a way.

develop: to bring something to existence through a temporally multistep activity.

development: the temporally multistep event by which something comes into existence.

die: to reach the end of life.

different: not identical with something, distinct from something, with an other identity (in relation to a specific entity).

difficult: something that requires a lot of strength or work.

direct: to cause the direction of movement of something.

direction: the line towards a goal or/and point.

disagreeable: causing dissatisfaction or disturbance to the condition of a living being.

distance: the length between two different locations in space.

distraction: the change in the direction of attention away from something and toward something else.

distress: the unpleasant emotional or feeling state of restlessness or/and pressure or/and inner conflict caused by something.

disturb: to not allow the natural or/and good state or happening of something to take place and be as it is.

disturbance: the not letting take place and the not letting being as it is of the natural or/and good state or happening of something.

disturbedness: the usually unpleasant unnatural state or happening of something.

do: to be purposefully active.

doubt: the feeling state that something is not as

perceived or/and as it appears or/and as it is presented.

down-to-earth: rooted in the intelligence of the laws of reality and thus of the laws of (human) life as well.

down-to-earthness: rootedness in the intelligence of the laws of reality and thus of the laws of life as well.

duty: the naturally felt or/and reflectively decided necessity to do something or/and be or/and behave in a specific way.

dwell: to remain.

dynamic: the property of intensity or/and strength enriched by one or more forces.

dynamics: the intensity or/and strength of a happening enriched by one or more forces.

dysschoolia: the weakness or difficulty in (a) being learning-inspiring and enabling learning-intelligence or/and (b) conveying learning content appropriately, i.e. in a recipient-centered manner.

earlier (1): further back in the past than something else.

earlier (2): in the past.

easy: something for which little force or labor is required.

ecology: the science (a) of the totality of the relationships of all living things to their living world and (b) of the totality of the effects of both on each other.

economy: the science of the totality of laws that determine and decide the control, preservation and (dynamic) development of resources within a given area.

education: the continuous and perpetual process of unfolding and developing human sensation, perception, thought, being and behavior.

effect (1): the change caused by something and felt by a living being.

effect (2): that which is there or happens directly and exclusively as a natural-law-result or/and personally felt result of something that is there or happens before.

effective: the composition of an activity or process by which a valuable result is caused or a meaningful purpose is fulfilled.

effectiveness: the degree of being effective of an activity or process.

eliminate: to bring something into non-existence or to take something away from one place and bring it to another.

emergence: the process by which something comes into existence.

emotion (1): a more or less pleasant or unpleasant powerful feeling.

emotion (2): inner energetic space, which results from a known or unknown reason/cause, and which, depending on the proportions and the kind of excitability, inertia and calmness, results in a certain mood/condition of the way of being or/and the readiness for activity and behavior of an evaluation-capable living being.

emotion (3): the more or less pleasant or unpleasant quality or inner existential atmosphere of the feeling state of a living being.

emotional: concerning the inner state of a living being caused by one or more emotions.

emotional intelligence: the experiential knowledge about the meaning of (especially) one's own emotions and the right way of dealing/being with them.

empathy: the ability to more or less feel the state of another living being.

empty: the property of containing nothing or containing nothing of something.

end (1): the last of several parts of a process or entity.

end (2): the location, point in space or point in time after which something is no longer there or does not longer exist.

endogenous: that which arises in an organism or a system from the organism's/system's own needs or necessities.

endomathemic: the term for the contents inherent in a matheme and their composition and organized arrangement determining this matheme.

energy (1): the total quantity of a substance which is or can be transformed to produce the movement or/and vibration of something.

energy (2): fuel or power.

energy (3): mysterious movedness from and within the "unbearable" fullness of the all-sustaining self-existence.

enlightenment (1): an intellectual movement and attitude (originated between the 17th and 18th century) that is based on rationality and autonomous thought, judgment and decision making.

enlightenment (2): holistic clarity.

enlightenment (3): holistic clarity, liberation and nourishment through the realization of the essence of reality.

entity: something that exists with its own independent identity in terms of substance or content.

equilibrium: the state of balance (Latin: aequi = equal + libra = weight).

estimate: to perceive the composition or/and significance or/and value of something.

ethics: the totality of all laws and rules that govern human action and behavior in interaction with others.

euphoria: very pleasant, self-affirming and self-willing state of a person or an other living being.

euphoric: being in a state of euphoria or containing euphoria.

eustress: the pleasant feeling state of restlessness or/and pressure caused by something, which moves a living being to sensible or/and pleasant action.

evolution: the temporally multistep event by which something comes into existence.

evolve: to come into being by a temporally multi-step activity.

exact: according in the smallest detail to a specification or expectation.

excited: being filled with uplifting and self-affirming strong inner stimulation.

excitement: feeling state of uplifting and self-affirming strong inner stimulation.

exercise: to use (repeatedly) physical or/and mental or/and emotional skills with the aim of maintaining or/and improving these skills.

exist: to occupy space grossly, subtly or transcendentally.

existence (1): the gross, subtle or transcendental occupation of space.

existence (2): the totality of everything that exists.

existence (3), or self-existence: that which exists by itself, that which needs nothing else as the cause of existence.

existence (4), or self-existence: the eternal; the infinite; the self-arising; that which gives rise, contains and constitutes the entire reality.

existence (root of our existence): the interface between existence itself and our psychophysical occurrence, happening and appearing. At this interface our existence begins, i.e. our consciousness that we are there. At the conscious beginning of our existence our most original touch of the totality of reality arises. From this touch and interaction with it, snapshots and patterns of impressions, needs and attitudes generate and form.

existential: everything that is decisive or/and significant for one's own existence (for one's own life).

exogenous: that which arises in an organism or a system not from the organism's/system's own needs or necessities.

exomathemic: the term for all circumstances, conditions and activities that are necessary for the learning of a matheme on the part and from the part of the learner.

experience (1): partial or total participation in a happening.

experience (2): conscious sensing and participating through organismic being touched by the existence, vibration and movement of reality.

experience: to participate in a being or/and happening in a sensing way.

explain: to show the reasons for something or the meaning or content of something.

explanation: showing the reasons for something or showing the meaning or content of something.

fact: the existence or being true of something.

false: not true.

family (1): a group of living beings that form a nourishing whole for biological or other important reasons.

family (2): group.

far: at a great distance.

fear: the oppressive and agonizing feeling that something that exists or is possible can cause disturbance, pain or non-existence.

feature: something that distinguishes an entity from one or more or all other entities.

feel (1): to sense.

feel (2): to sense an emotion.

feel (3): to sense an intuition.

feeling (1): the sensed or felt inner state of a person or other living being.

feeling (2): emotion.

feeling (3): intuition.

feeling (4): faculty of sentient perception and cognition.

feeling faculty: the capability of feeling.

fill: to cause something to become full of something else.

focal point: the important or more important center of a context of content.

focus (1): the point or area to which one's attention is directed.

focus (2): to direct one's attention to a point or area.

follow: to be or happen further or farther in time or space than something else.

following (1): being or happening directly, solely, and exclusively later in time or space than something that is or happens before.

following (2): being or happening coincidentally later in time or space than something that is or happens before.

force (1): directed energy producing motion or vibration.

force (2): high degree of motion or vibration producing directed physical or also mental or emotional energy of a living being or something else.

force (3): power or influence capacity of something.

form: the way of coherent arrangement of the components of something.

form (1): to create.

form (2): to create an overall form from certain parts.

free: the quality of the feeling state in which we feel no internal or external constraints or/and limitations or restrictions or/and necessities.

freedom: the feeling state in which we feel no internal or external constraints or/and limitations or restrictions or/and necessities.

freedom, organismic: the state in which we exist as a free self and feel the unhindered realization of our actualizing tendency.

"Truth is a shining goddess, always veiled, always distant, never wholly approachable, but worthy of all the devotion of which the human spirit is capable."

Bertrand Russell

From **'friendship'**

to **'necessity'**

friendship: a relationship between two people containing trust, affection and love for each other.

fulfill: to cause completely the condition for an existence or for something to happen.

fulfilled: being full of something.

fulfillment (1): the existing of something after the conditions for it have been caused.

fulfillment (2): emotional nourishment.

full: the quality of containing something to the highest possible degree.

fully: in a high or in the highest degree of something.

future: the time when (compared to the present) everything will be there that has not yet been there, and everything will yet happen that has not yet happened.

future: everything that has not yet been there and will be there, and everything that has not yet happened and will happen.

gas: finest and not solid or liquid materiality.

genesis: the process by which something comes into existence.

goal: the final state or place of a movement or action.

good: sufficient to very high degree of something that fulfills a purpose.

grief: inwardly felt depressing and crushing energy, usually due to a deficiency, the removal of which would complete a contented wholeness.

ground: the lowest surface or level of something in space.

group: a number of two or more living things or other entities that are together, come together or are perceived together as a unit by some common characteristic.

grow: to be in the process of reaching a higher degree in one or more properties.

happen: to be in motion or/and change.

happening: being in motion or change of one or more entities.

happiness: the feeling state filled with a high or highest degree of satisfaction and euphoria.

harmonious: anything that is either a part of or a contribution to a harmony.

harmony: the state of the composition and arrangement of something that gives rise to the feeling state of smoothness and contentment.

healing: the event leading into undisturbedness, wholeness and liberation.

heavy: something that has a lot of weight.

holistic: all-encompassing, concerning the whole (of something) (holon = the whole).

homeostasis: the process of self-regulation to maintain the same state (Greek: homöo = same, stasis = state).

human: an organism biologically-anatomically belonging to the Homo sapiens species and possessing sensation, reason and intelligence of speech.

I/self: the energy expansion of a sufficiently developed organism receiving/including everything perceived and experienced, and experiencing itself as its own identity.

identical: just as.

identity: the spatiotemporally-uniquely arranged or configured unified form of energy or existence that makes something exactly what it is.

image: something that, by its appearance or occurrence, shows the identity of the content of something else.

image: to reflect or/and represent the identity of the content of something by the appearance or occurrence of something else.

importance: the composition or/and quality of something, determined by the degree to which it fulfills a need or necessity.

important: something that has importance.

information (1): the content of a meaning-bearing part of reality.

information (2): energy being in a certain form.

insight: spontaneously arising content of knowledge, cognition, understanding or thinking.

instinct: an innate or strongly internalized way of sensing, perceiving, acting or/and behaving.

intelligence (1): naturally available or retrievable stored knowledge coupled with the ability to see through, understand, figure out, learn, know something new for oneself and in its possible relationships to others.

intelligence (2): knowledge or/and information.

intense: powerful.

interest: the feeling state of motivatedness towards something.

interested: being in the feeling state of motivatedness towards something.

internalize: to make something a unified and no longer separable part of one's total being and capability, through experience, practice or learning.

interpersonal: pertaining to the psychophysical happenings between persons.

interrelation: the composition of the link or/and relationship of something with something else.

intimacy: the high to very high degree of personal openness in being with others, arising from experientially real trust.

intrapersonal: concerns the psychophysical happening within a person.

intuition: deeper, pre-reflected and consciously not further determinable sensation, perception or/and knowledge.

joy: internally felt euphoric energy.

joyful: inwardly permeated and suffused with euphoric vitality.

judge: to form or show a judgment.

judgment: (well-)founded opinion or decision about something.

justify: to state or show the (reasonable) cause or triggering event for something.

kind: totality of properties.

knowledge (1): naturally available and to-some-thing-enabling living information or totality of information.

knowledge (2): the totality of everything a living being learned or/and experienced.

language (1): the totality of all content that can be communicated through speaking and writing.

language (2): the (human) ability to communicate content through speaking and writing.

language (3): a system of communication.

language intelligence: the mastery of appropriate words and forms of expression to describe content of perceiving, feeling, experiencing, thinking and knowing.

later: further ahead in the future than something else.

law(s) of humans: manner of conduct decided and established by nature or human beings and binding on all concerned.

law(s) of nature or reality: the unchanging way something exists and behaves.

learning: the process or experience that leads to new knowledge or/and being.

learning (autotelic learning): learning activity that is itself already the goal or/and fulfillment of its happening.

learning (organismic learning): change of knowledge or/and being determined by the total-organismic intelligence and generated by total-organismic experience.

learning cybernetics: the equilibrial control of the unmistaken direction of the learning process.

learning economy: for effective learning it is necessary that the investment of time and energy in learning something is guided by what is the simplest way of learning that something, if (1) by 'simple' is meant what is really necessary, and no more or less, and (2) the composition of the simplest is determined by all the relevant endo- and exomathemic components.

learning goal: the new state of knowing and/or being to be achieved through a learning process.

learning intelligence (1): the masterful knowledge of how learning works.

learning intelligence (2): the ability to (1) holistically recognize, perceive, feel and understand (1.1) one's authentic motivation, (1.2) authentic reality, and (1.3) the relationship of one's authentic motivation to authentic reality, (2) fully design a living strategy to harmonize this relationship, and (3) steadfastly implement and fulfill the designed strategy.

length: the how much of something between its beginning and its end.

life (1): the total time of the life of an organism.

life (2): existence, the fact of conscious experience.

life (3): general term for inherently purposeful, self-organizing, metabolizing and reproducing bodies, entities or beings capable of change, sensation and motion or/and growth.

life force: the force that vitalizes a living being.

life mastery: the sufficient, complete or very high ability to (a) fulfill the necessities of life and (b) to realize as many valuable possibilities inherent in life as is feasible and appropriate.

life skill: one of the skills necessary for a realized and contented life.

light: something that has little weight.

line: the length which connects two points different from each other.

linguistics: the science of the origin, function and modes of use of language.

little: indicates a small amount of something.

liveliness: vitality.

living being: an inherently purposeful, self-organizing, metabolizing and reproducing organism capable of change, sensation and motion or/and growth.

location: a part, area or point within space or a room.

logic (1): well-founded and soundly inferred correctness.

logic (2): the meaningful inner structure of a fact, circumstance, happening or action.

logical: anything that has a logic.

loneliness: the emotional and existential state of abandoned aloneness.

long: greater in length than necessary or appropriate.

longing: deeper, very strong and the essence of a living being decisively touching need to be somehow or/and to experience something.

love (1): affection for something that is pleasant.

love (2): related or unrelated to someone or something (1) unconditional, (2) containing, nurturing, and dissolving one's self, (3) basic-existentially blissful and "unbearably" ecstatic infinity of feeling and being a yes.

love (being in love): being within, permeated by and nourished by love.

loved (or being loved): the nourishment state of being certain of being loved by one or more living beings.

luck: good or right conditions for something.

lust: wanting filled with euphoria.

machine: created material structure, which fulfills a work by force or energy.

make (1): to create.

make (2): to cause.

manifestation (1): a particular form of energy that has been created.

manifestation (2): free and bound energy emerged from the mystery.

master: a person with a complete or very high ability in something.

master (1): to be able to do or finish something difficult.

master (2): to keep something under control.

masterful: like a master.

mastery: the sufficient, complete, strong or very high ability in something.

mathematics: the quantifying of reality and the living world, the transforming of both into sizes, quantities and measures, in order to (computationally) achieve different and diverse goals in both areas.

matheme: in itself complete meaningful part of a learning content.

mathetics: the science of learning (manthanein = to learn).

matter: concentration of physical-chemical elements.

mean: to have an opinion.

meaning (1): the content that a living being associates with an object or with anything in particular at all.

meaning (2): the content of something shown by a linguistic or other sign or symbol.

meaning (3): importance.

meaningful (1): something that has an intelligible or/and logical meaning.

meaningful (2): important.

meaning of life (1): the purpose of life itself.

meaning of life (2): the purpose of an individual life based on one's own design.

meaning of life (3): the purpose of an individual life on the basis of one's own actualizing tendency.

meaning of life (4): the purpose inherent in life of unfolding and realizing or actualizing the powers and dispositions that constitute life within and as an expression and happening of the most holistic pure reality possible.

means: something by which something else can be accomplished.

measure: to find out how much something is when compared with something of its kind.

medicine: research and study of true knowledge of the proper and good maintenance, nourishment and functioning of all living organisms.

meditate (1): to reflect quietly and deeply.

meditate (2): to gather all one's own active organismic powers and immerse them in reality in order to obtain or/and attain mental clarity or/and mental or/and spiritual nourishment.

mental: everything that is perceptible, experience-able and thinkable through inner perceptual contents.

mind: the total mental faculty consisting of perceiving, understanding and judging.

mixture: being together of two or more kinds of substance.

mostly: the between very large to largest number of the happening or being there of something.

motion: the change in location of something, caused by a force, to a different location distanced from the first.

motivatedness: the sensation of a need-generated restlessness.

motivation: a feeling state in which a moving force (originating from a motivatedness) towards something is sensed.

motivational intelligence: (a) the experiential knowledge of one's needs and (b) the sense of real life necessities coupled with (c) the ability to fulfill both.

movedness: being in a state of motion toward something.

much: indicates the large amount or number of something.

music: arrangement of sounds causing emotions and inner feeling states.

must: to be an irresistibly inseparable part of a movement or a current of force towards something.

mystery (1): that which remains hidden from our knowing ability.

mystery (2) of all existence: the unknown and inexplicable, out of which all manifested being, all energy and all space originate.

natural: corresponding to and completely coinciding with the nature of something.

nature: the origin of something and the unchangeable laws of its happening and existing.

navigate: to determine the manner and direction of movement/change of something from one place/location/state to another place/location/state.

near: at a small distance.

necessary: the designation of something that must happen or be there in order for something else to happen or be there.

necessity: that which must happen or be there in order for something else to happen or be there.

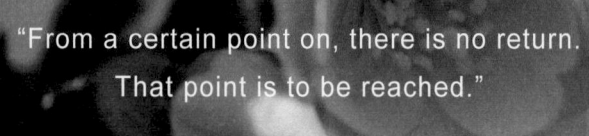

"From a certain point on, there is no return.
That point is to be reached."

Franz Kafka

From **'need'**

to **'satisfaction'**

need: the feeling of a state of deficiency and a consequent restlessness and a simultaneous directedness towards the elimination of this deficiency.

need: to feel a state of deficiency and a consequent restlessness and a simultaneous directedness towards the elimination of this deficiency.

negate: to feel or show negation.

negation (1): showing perception of something as false or untrue.

negation (2): the sensing or showing of not wanting to be with something.

negative: causing negation.

new: having existed for a short time.

no: expression of negation.

normal: something that is in its characteristics (most of the time, generally) as expected by others.

not: indicating the absence of existence, truth, validity or taking place of something.

nourish: to give appropriate food for health and growth to a living being.

nourishment: the state in which a living being is provided with all the substances necessary for the completeness of its existence and for its resting and contented wholeness.

number: the totality of how often (more than once) something is there in time or space.

nutrition: all substances necessary for the existence or/and for the growth and for the resting and contented wholeness of a living being.

obligation: the feeling of a duty.

observation: attentive or/and exact, and usually connected with a purpose, perception of something.

observe: to perceive something attentively or/and accurately, and usually with a purpose.

obvious: the quality of being perceptually or/and feelingly or/and intuitively completely clear, undeniable and unclouded.

often: the great number of the happening or being there of something.

old: everything that is (very) progressed in the length of its existence.

ontic (1): the attribute of actually existing.

ontic (2): the quality of knowing something that becomes possible or is there through the being (in one's own being) of that something.

opinion: a person's specific perception or/and specific understanding or/and specific conviction related to something.

opportunity: time and space for the possibility of something.

order (1): the way something accidentally or purposefully is or becomes arranged.

order (2): the composition and set-up of one or more elements required by a particular system.

order (3): the appropriate condition or/and composition of an entity.

organ: an in itself complete, integrated and a specific function fulfilling part of a living being.

organism: a living being or a complex living system consisting of interrelated elements whose properties and relationships to each other are "decided" by a purpose-determining (existence-determining) compass serving the living being/system as a whole and inherent in it.

organismic: belonging to or pertaining to an organism.

organismic intelligence: the knowledge and capacity generated from feeling the effect of all happening or all intake of different psychophysical nourishment on the health and contentment of a living being as a whole and not on only one of all aspects that constitute a living being as an organism.

organismicity: organismic reality, potentiality and intelligence.

organization (1): the act of organizing or/and an organizing happening or the state of being organized.

organization (2): a group of living beings that relate to and act with each other in such a way as to accomplish a specific purpose or achieve a specific goal.

organize: to bring a system into such a favorable coherent arrangement that this system has a fluid functionality or all the characteristics of a healthy living organism, so that a certain purpose is fulfilled or a certain goal is achieved.

other: an entity with the not (unique) own identity or with an identity existing in a spatial distance.

pain: physical or/and psychological agonizing state difficult or very difficult to bear.

parents (1): the living beings through which a new living being comes into existence biologically.

parents (2): the living beings who have the responsibility for another living being until it becomes independent in life.

part: one of two or more entities that, taken together, are a whole.

participate: to exist within a state, being or/and

happening.

passion: strong to very strong feeling power for something.

passionate: filled with feeling power to a high degree.

past: the time when (compared to the present) everything was already there or everything has already happened.

past: everything that was already there or everything that has already happened.

perceive: to consciously notice objects or elements of external or internal reality in their identity in a more or less concrete way by means of sentient faculties, such as the senses.

perception: the bipolar event by which a subject, i.e. a psychophysical recipient, becomes aware of the identity of objects or elements of external or internal reality in a more or less concrete way by means of sentient faculties, such as the senses.

period: a smaller or larger part of time, a smaller or

larger part of the "length" of the existence of something or of the "length" of a happening.

person: a dignity-bearing and freedom-feeling human being.

phenomenological: the dimension of the experienced, as this appears to us (subjectively) consciously.

philosophy: the love for wisdom.

physical: bodily or/and material.

physics: exploration and study of true knowledge (a) of the nature of matter, energy and all forces, and (b) of all laws of existence and behavior of these.

place: a part, area or point within space or a room or a specific field.

plan: a thought-out system by which something is to be or can be achieved.

plan: to bring a plan into existence.

play: an activity (very often determined in its happening also by rules) which causes joy or/and satisfaction.

play: to participate in an activity (very often determined in its happening also by rules) which causes joy or/and satisfaction.

pleasant: causing satisfaction or contentment.

pleasure: sensation filled with euphoria.

positive (1): causing affirmation.

positive (2): the quality of being good or useful for something.

possibility (1): something that is possible.

possibility (2): a means.

possible: anything for whose existence there are causes or causes are conceivable.

practice: repeated application of physical or/and mental or/and emotional skills with the aim of preserving or improving these skills.

practice: to do something longer and repeatedly in order to become better or very good at it.

pragmatism: the ability or/and way to orient and adapt to real situations and to the knowledge of how these can lead to success when there are problems to solve or goals to achieve.

precise: in every smallest detail in accordance with a requirement or expectation.

presence: the time in which what is there right now is there, and in which what is happening right now is happening (and not what has already been there and has happened, and not what will still be there or will still happen).

present: what is there and happening right now (and not what has been there or has happened, and not what will be there or is yet to happen).

prioritize: to list the stages of a multi-stage event or the individual items on a list in terms of their priority.

priority: coming first before something else.

problem: small to high degree of interference or disturbance with the happening or existence of something.

process: a multi-stage happening.

property: quality or/and characteristic.

psychic: mental-emotional.

psychophysical: mental-emotional-physical.

purpose: the goal of an action or happening or process.

quality: the degree of the property or/and composition of something that serves a purpose.

quantification: the act of quantifying.

quantify (1): to turn something into quantity or quantities.

quantify (2): to perceive something transformed into sizes, quantities and measures.

quantity: the number or amount of something.

rational: possessing the property or ability of inferential reasoning.

rationality: the property or ability of inferential reasoning.

reach: to arrive at a place or time through movement or/and through a process.

read: to experience the content of a text through understanding.

real: everything that exists.

realism: the ability or/and way to perceive things as they really are, without becoming or/and being influenced by beliefs, wishful thinking, uncertainty and hope.

reality: the totality of everything that exists.

realize (1): to recognize.

realize (2): to actualize something or cause something to come into real existence.

reason (1): the cause or initiating happening or initiating being for something.

reason (2): the ability of logical thinking, understanding and judging.

reasonable (1): something that is logical or/and sensible.

reasonable (2): something that is appropriate in part or in whole to achieve a purpose.

receive (1): to accept something given.

receive (2): to let something into one's own open sensing space.

receptive: being open for something to come into one's own sensing space.

recognize: to perceive something in its identity.

reflect: to think with the aim of finding out or/and understanding something.

relation: the way something is related or connected to something else or the way things or entities are related or connected to each other.

relationship: the way of connectedness between something and something else.

relaxation: the freeing of the inner energy flow from being held and pressed.

relaxation intelligence: the experiential knowledge of the different dimensions and the corresponding fulfillment processes of (a) one's nourishment and (b) the real necessities of life.

relaxedness: the feeling state of freedom from holding and pressing of the inner energy flow and condition.

reliability: perceived certainty of the immutability of something.

reliable: the property (of something) of being perceived as unchangeable.

remain: to be unchanged for an (indefinitely) longer period of time in one place or state or/and happening.

representation: the presentation of something by means of a plane/dimension other than that to which this something belongs.

responsibility: the natural or otherwise established right or authorization for something, i.e. the authoritative and committing authorship for something.

responsible: being in charge of something for which authorship naturally belongs to someone or is assigned by other arrangements.

rest: the state of being undisturbed or/and motionless.

restlessness: the state of prolonged or/and permanent inner disturbance or/and disturbing agitation.

result: that which is there or happens (directly and exclusively) next, after something that is there before or happens before.

right (1): true.

right (2): good or/and appropriate.

rule: humanly decided and determined binding manner of behavior for all involved.

sadness: inwardly felt depressing and crushing energy, usually due to a deficiency, the removal of which would complete a contented wholeness.

safety: being in a/the state free from (or without) danger.

satisfaction: euphorically satiating state of a person or of a living being, which arises from the fulfillment of a need.

"Nothing can be added to or taken away from the Divine. It cannot be invoked or worshipped with flowers and leaves. Meditations and mantras cannot reach it. How could it be worshipped as supreme? For in It, there are neither differences nor unity."

Avadhuta Gita

From **'school'**

to **'young'**

school: physical or content location of schooling.

schooling: acting in such a way that a human being or a living being receives learning-intelligent help, support, accompaniment or/and knowledge in and about how to realize one's own learning needs or necessities in an organismically wise way.

schooling intelligence: the ability to educate others in an enthusiastic, learning-intelligent, interpersonal-learning-intelligent and recipient-centered manner.

science: activity dedicated to the "generation" or/and discovery of true knowledge.

scientific: anything dedicated to the "generation" or/and discovery of true knowledge.

self/I: the energy expansion of a sufficiently developed organism receiving/including everything perceived and experienced and experiencing itself as its own identity.

self-aware: the state in which an organism includes itself within the radius of its consciousness or attention.

self-awareness: the self-feeling of an I.

self-confidence: the strong sense of one's own valuable abilities, characteristics and qualities.

self-esteem: the degree of experientially confirmed importance or/and satisfaction with oneself.

self-love: self-related (1) unconditional, (2) containing, nourishing and dissolving one's own I, (3) basic-existential-blissful and "unbearably"-blissful yes-infinity.

self-sufficiency: being independent from others in the way to live and to exist and in causing all the necessary resources for life.

self-sufficient: to be independent from others in the way to live and to exist and in causing all the necessary resources for life.

sense (1): ability of sensation and perception associated with an organ of a living being.

sense (2): meaning or content of something.

sense (1): to be touched or filled by the senses or

by an inner energy.

sense (2): to notice an energetic arrangement or transformation psychically or/ and physically.

sense (3): to feel something (more) subtly or most subtly in unobstructed consciousness.

sensing: ability of subtler and deeper feeling perception and recognition of something that is not directly or easily perceptible and recognizable.

sentence (1): complete meaningful linguistic information.

sentence (2): a interrelated group of words containing a subject and a verb.

sequence: the manner of arrangement of two or more things or entities following each other in a series.

series: the totality of at least two or more things or entities following one another in space, time or content.

set (1): a number of distinct entities.

set (2): totality of different elements perceived as a whole.

short: smaller in length than necessary or appropriate.

should: to be obliged, to be asked or to feel/recognize the necessity to do or/and to be something.

sign: something that shows something else in terms of content.

significance: importance.

significant: having important meaning or/and meaningfulness or showing an important content (signum = sign, significare = to show).

skill: a higher or very high degree of an ability to do something.

small: low degree of (usually) length.

solution: the way of elimination of a problem or difficulty.

solve (1): to eliminate a problem or difficulty.

solve (2): to find out the way for achieving a goal.

space (1): the infinity that contains everything.

space (2): an empty content partially or totally enclosed by something.

spell: to have the ability of writing words in the sequence of letters that make them up.

spelling: the ability of writing words in the sequence of letters that make them up.

spirit (1): the sensed feeling that permeates and fills a particular area.

spirit (2): the unbound acting force or power or energy of the essence of reality.

spontaneity: the feeling state in which free, unplanned, natural and authentic experiencing and acting take place.

spontaneous: free, unplanned, natural, authentic, by itself.

start: to cause the beginning of an existence or an

event.

state: the composition and way of being or existing of someone or something.

state of affairs: the state of the entities that are important or determining for the existence or/and happening of something and their relationship to each other.

step: a segment of progressing or coming closer to a goal.

straight: in the shortest length between two points in space.

strategy: the being organized of a process that leads or should or can lead to the achievement of a goal.

strength (1): high degree of force or power.

strength (2): the degree of the ability to be active.

stress: the feeling state caused by something and consequently characterized by restlessness or/and pressure/tension or/and conflict.

strong (1): containing high degree of force or power.

strong (2): the degree of someone's ability to be active.

structure: the particular way in which all the elements of a system are related or connected to each other.

subject (1): the psychophysical receiver of experience inside the consciousness of a sufficiently developed living organism.

subject (2): the part (the word or group of words) in a sentence from which the content of a verb comes.

success: the good or/and valuable result of an activity or a process.

successful: the property of an activity or process that brings about success.

suffer: to feel pain or to be in unpleasant feeling states in a high to very high degree.

suffering: that which causes a high to very high degree of feeling pain or being in unpleasant feeling states.

symbol: sign.

system: a unified whole consisting of interrelated parts.

tangible: anything that can be perceived and experienced by the senses.

technique: the structure and composition and totality of the steps of a process or/and of a purposeful activity.

technology: the structure, composition and operational way of a machine or machines in general.

tension: a feeling state in which the internal energy flow is held and pressed.

terminate: to cause the end of an existence or happening.

text: written reproduction of a content by a series of coherent well-ordered and meaningful sentences.

think: to be purposefully mentally active.

thinking: purposeful mental activity.

thought: a (more ore less complete in itself) content in thinking.

time: the "length" of the existence of something or the "length" of a happening.

to: shows a certain direction or goal.

together: being within the presence or space of one or more persons or entities or things.

togetherness: to be so connected with or to be within the presence or space of one or more living beings, persons or entities or things, in a way, that instead of the feeling of being alone, there is or arises the sensed being part of a greater whole.

transform: to change the composition or/and the shape or/and the structure or/and the essence or/and the identity of something.

transformation: the process by which something comes into a new composition or/and shape or/and structure or/and essence or/and identity.

trauma: longer-lasting mental-emotional wound usually caused by a life-threatening or/and strong-pain-creating situation.

true (1): everything that is real.

true (2): everything that coincides with reality.

trust (1): the emotionally-mentally deep (and nurturing) state of knowledge and certainty toward a person or anything else at all, which is unmistakably reliable or/and benevolent in its true being and behavior toward the trusting person.

trust (2): sensed certainty of the correctness, truth or/and reliability of something.

truth (1): a property of the real.

truth (2): the coincidence of a statement or information or of a happening with reality.

understanding: the perceiving or/and sensing or/and becoming of the identity, meaning, content or/and essence of something.

unique: occupying only one single location in space or existing once in a specific field.

unity (1): the sensed or in an other way constituted oneness of two or more living beings or other entities with each other.

unity (2): a fixed quantity that is being used for measurement.

universe: the totality of all existence.

untrue: not true.

use: to transform something into the means of a purposeful action.

utilize: to transform something into a means for something else.

valuable: the high degree of importance that something has for a living being.

value: the degree of importance something has for a living being.

verb: the part of speech usually denoting a happening or activity.

very: to a high to highest degree.

vibration: fast to very (imperceptibly) rapid move-ment of something swinging back and forth at a small distance.

vital: having a lot of energy.

vitality: the feeling state of being bodily permeat-ed and uplifted by a significant or high degree of energy.

voluntary: pertaining to one's own and free will or/ and motivatedness.

want: to feel motivational energy towards the fulfill-ment of a need.

wanting, true: real wanting that leads to action. We cannot feel it and remain passive and inactive at the same time. We recognize true wanting by restless-ness. When I really want something, I recognize it by the fact that I become restless when I do not yet have or am not yet what I want. So restless that I automatically give in to the urge to move, which generates the necessary action that leads me to what I want.

way: set of properties that determine how something happens or exists.

whole (1): something in which nothing necessary for its own existence is missing.

whole (2): something that exists in the completeness and indivisibility of its nature and purpose of existence.

whole (1): the quality of being such that everything necessary for one's existence is there and nothing is lacking.

whole (2): the quality in which something exists in the completeness and indivisibility of its nature and purpose of existence.

whole (being whole): the shining of one's own nature and purposefullness of existence.

wholeness: the quality or property of existing in the completeness and undividedness of one's own nature and existential purposefullness.

wholly: in a high or in the highest degree of something.

will: the directed total force that drives a living being to a mode of existence or/and being or/and effective action and arises from and through all respective needs.

wisdom: deeper to most profound knowledge acquired through experience and understanding.

with: within the presence or space of one or more persons or entities or things.

wonder: something that, by its inexplicably very strong properties, causes a holistically sensed deep and pleasantly captivating feeling state.

word: the smallest part of language that can be spoken or written and that shows the content or meaning of something.

work (1): a purposeful activity.

work (2): a purposeful activity that is paid.

work (3): something accomplished by persons or

living beings or also created by them (or by nature).

world: everything that exists and that in which it exists.

worry: the feeling of uneasiness or/and anxiety caused by a (possible) problem or danger.

wound: physical or/and mental disturbance or injury that causes pain.

wrong: not good or/and not appropriate.

yes (1): the expression of perceiving something as right or true.

yes (2): the expression of feeling and showing of wanting to be together with something.

young: not (at all) long after the beginning of the existence of something.

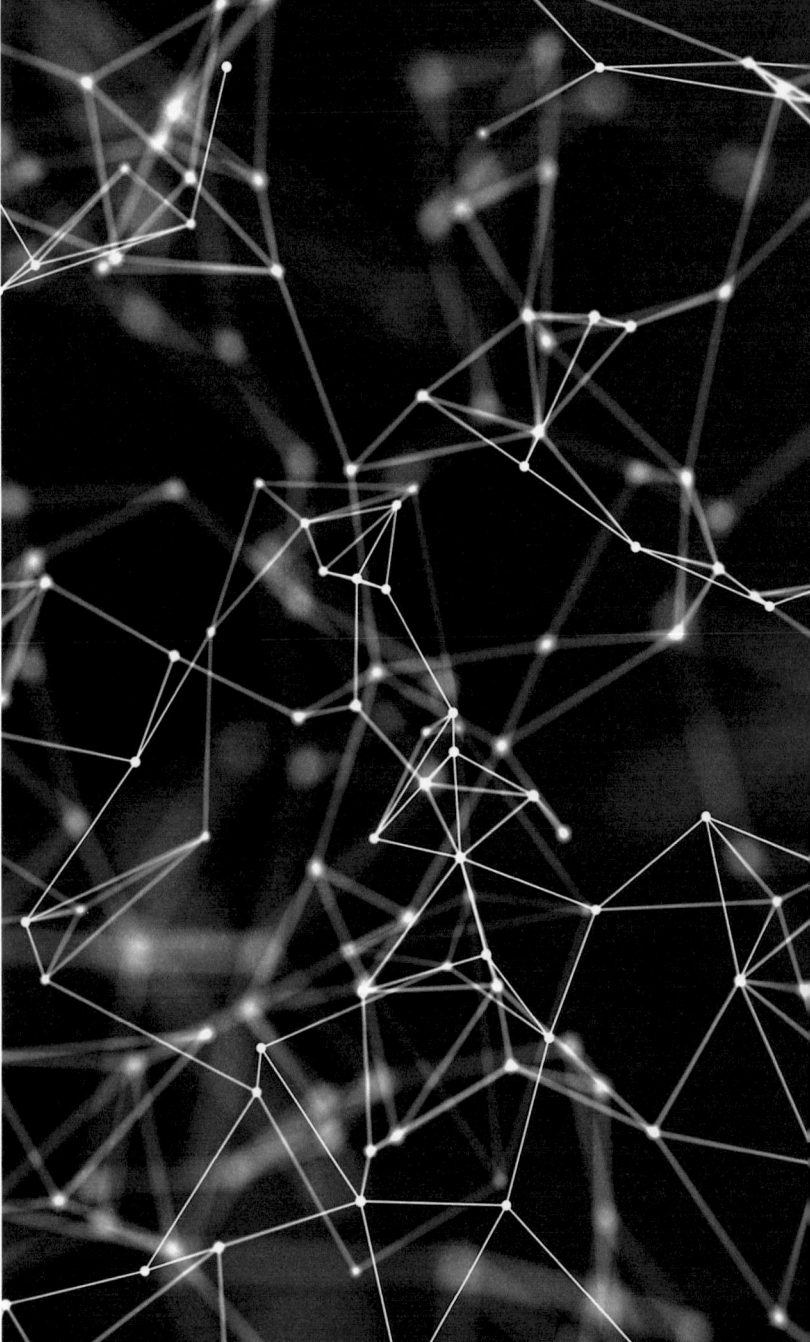

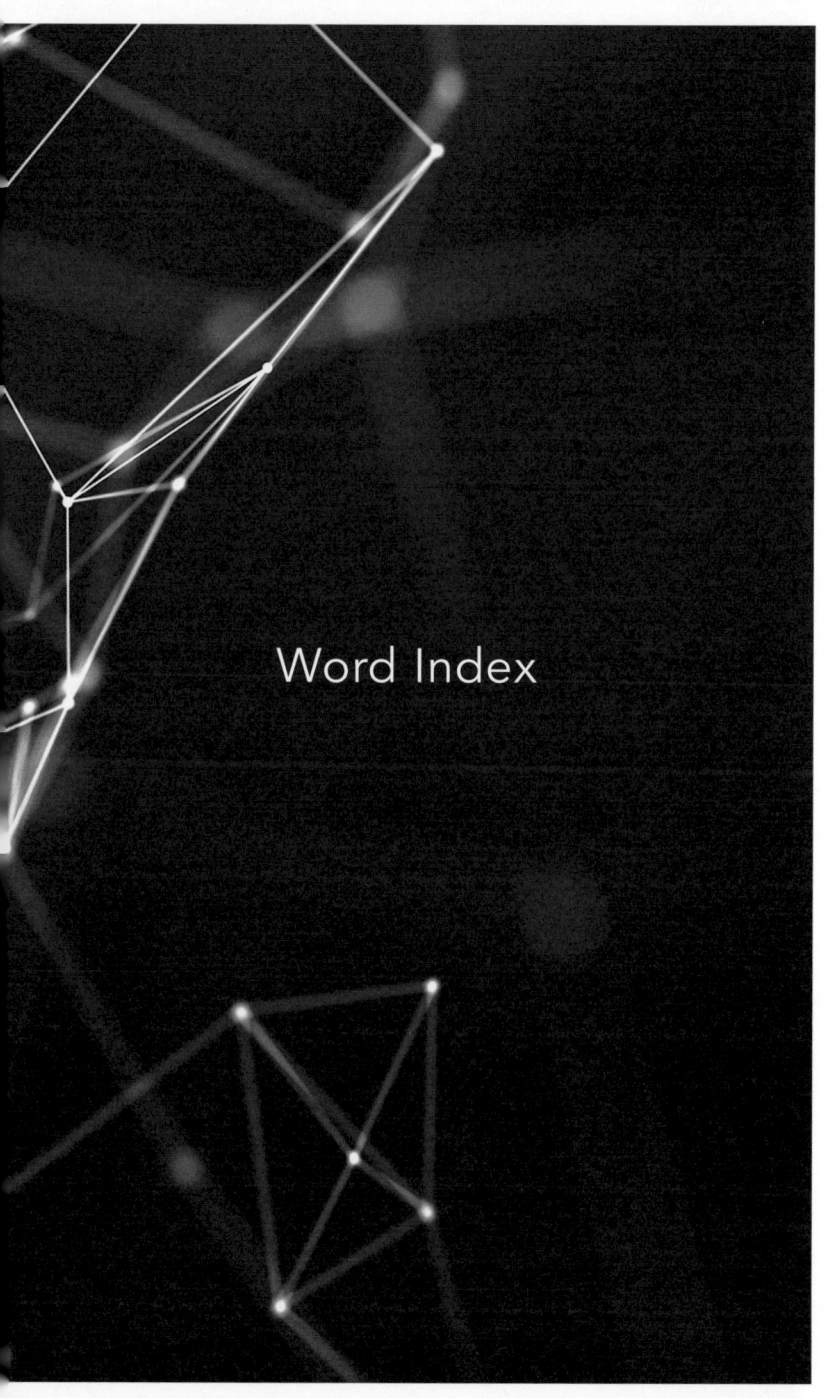

Word Index

A

B

C

D

F

G

H

I

J

K

L

M

matheme - 89

mathetics - 89

matter - 90

mean - 90

meaning (1) - 90

meaning (2) - 90

meaning (3) - 90

meaningful (1) - 90

meaningful (2) - 90

meaning of life (1) - 90

meaning of life (2) - 90

meaning of life (3) - 90

meaning of life (4) - 91

means - 91

measure - 91

medicine - 91

meditate (1) - 91

meditate (2) - 91

mental - 91

mind - 92

mixture - 92

mostly - 92

motion - 92

motivatedness - 92

motivation - 92

motivational intelligence - 92

movedness - 92

N

nourish - 100

nourishment - 100

number - 100

nutrition - 100

O

---

obligation - 100

observation - 100

observe - 100

obvious - 100

often - 101

old - 101

ontic (1) - 101

ontic (2) - 101

opinion - 101

opportunity - 101

order (1) - 101

order (2) - 101

order (3) - 101

organ - 102

organism - 102

organismic - 102

organismic intelligence - 102

P

Q

R

S

T

U

Y

Quotations And Sources Of Reference

In the order in which they appear in this book

---

14   *The world is everything:* from **Tractatus logico-philo-
sophicus** by **Ludwig Wittgenstein**, 1921.

21   *Thus, I have a completely:* from **Brief an Oldenburg**
(Letter to Oldenburg) by **Benedictus de Spinoza**, in
Baruch de Spinoza: Briefwechsel (Correspondence),
edited by Manfred Walther, lines 17-22, Nov.-Dec.
1675.

23   *Though the Logos:* **Heraclitus, Fragments, DK, B2.**

57   *The Present is always there:* from **Die Welt als Wille
und Vorstellung** (The World as Will and Representation) by **Arthur Schopenhauer**, first volume, §54.

74   *Truth is a shining:* from **University Education** in **Fact
and Fiction** by **Bertrand Russell,** London 1961.

96   *From a certain point:* from **"Du bist die Aufgabe":
Aphorismen** ("You are the task": Aphorisms) by **Franz
Kafka**, Göttingen 2019.

114 *Nothing can be added to:* from **Avadhuta Gita**,
chapter 4, verse 1.

Publisher: Ioannis Tzivanakis Verlag, Hamburg 2021.

Printed in Germany.

ISBN 978-3-940493-35-4

www.lexiconoflife.net

Bibliographic information published by the Deutsche
Nationalbibliothek (German National Library): The Deutsche
Nationalbibliothek lists this publication in the Deutsche
Nationalbibliografie (German National Bibliography).

Other Publications

By Ioannis Tzivanakis

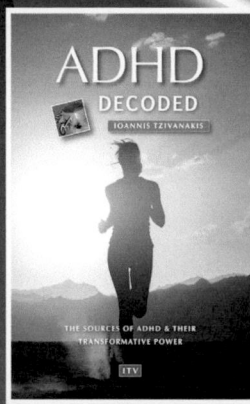

About The Author

Ioannis Tzivanakis studied linguistics and philosophy of language at the University of Bremen. His focus was on *semantics*, *consciousness research* and *wholeness*.

Since 1996 he has worked as a trainer, coach and counselor in the areas of *learning intelligence, ADHD, life counseling and spirituality* both in Germany and worldwide.

In 2006 and 2007 he published four issues of the *Learning Intelligence Magazine* on foundations of *learning*, *learning intelligence*, *management* and *spirituality*.

In 2018 his book "ADHD decoded" was published and in 2021 his writings "Attention Counseling" and "learnfree".

Further information can be found on the Internet:
www.tzivanakis.com